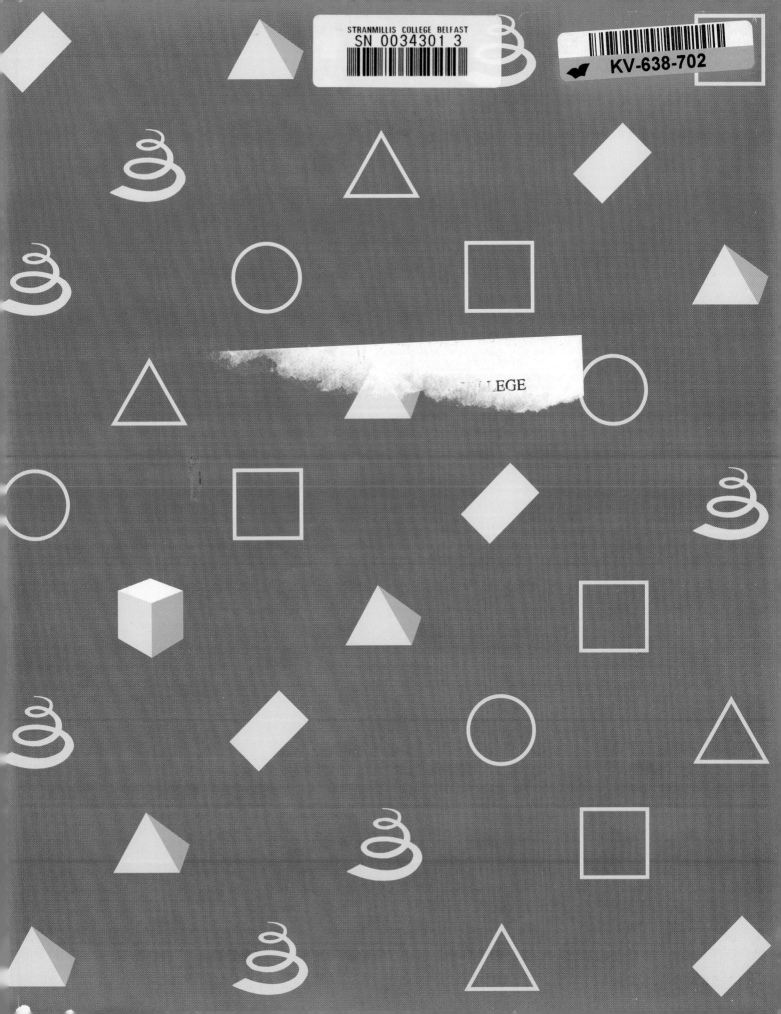

TRIANGLES AND PYRAMIDS

Sally Morgan

Wayland

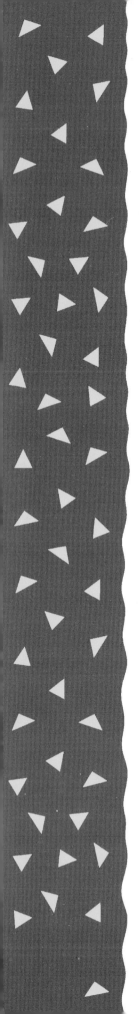

The World of Shapes

Circles and Spheres
Spirals
Squares and Cubes
Triangles and Pyramids

Series editor: Joanna Bentley
Book editor: Marcella Forster
Series designer: The Pinpoint Design Company

First published in 1994 by Wayland (Publishers) Ltd,
61 Western Road, Hove, East Sussex BN3 1JD, England

British Library Cataloguing in Publication Data
Morgan, Sally
Triangles and Pyramids. — (World of Shapes Series)
I. Title   II. Series
516.15   CD. V

ISBN 0 7502 1283 7

Typeset by Dorchester Typesetting Group Ltd, Dorset, England
Printed and bound in Italy by Canale, C.S.p.A.

Contents

What is a triangle?

A triangle is a shape that has three sides. The three sides are joined together to make three corners.

In the photographs below there are examples of different types of triangle.

Different types of triangle

All triangles have three sides, but they do not all have exactly the same shape. The lengths of the sides may **differ**. There are three types of triangle.

There are triangles which have sides that are all the same length. These are called equilateral triangles. ▶

◀ Some triangles have two sides the same length but the third side is a different length. It may be longer or shorter. These are called isosceles triangles.

The third type of triangle, in which all three sides are different lengths, is called a scalene triangle. ▼

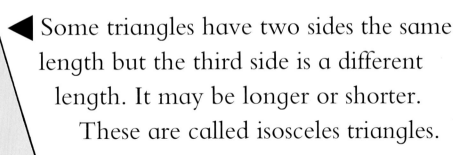

Measuring triangles

In the photographs on this page you will find many triangles.

Use a ruler to measure the sides of some of the triangles. Make a note of the measurements. Look at your measurements and see if you can work out which type of triangle each one is.

Fitting triangles together

When triangles of the same size are placed side by side, they fit closely together. There are no spaces in between. Several triangles can be placed side by side to make other shapes. Four isosceles triangles placed together make a square.

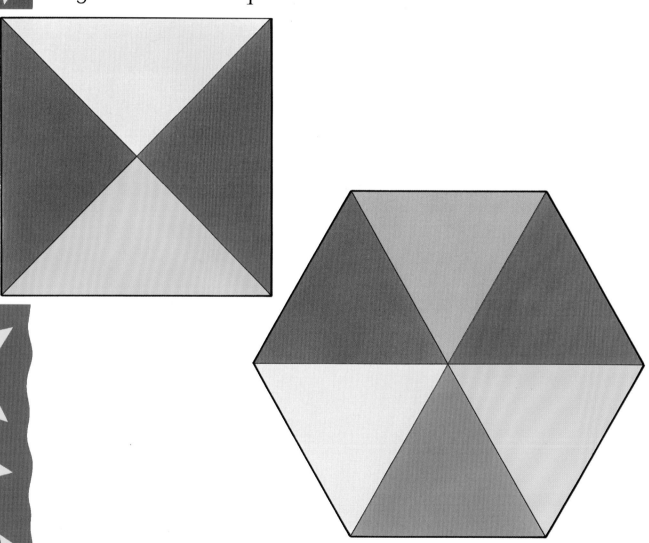

When six equilateral triangles are placed together they can make a hexagon, a shape that has six equal sides.

Trace the triangle below on to a piece of card six times. Cut out the six triangles.

Using the cards, try to make the following shapes. First, make one large triangle from four of the cards.

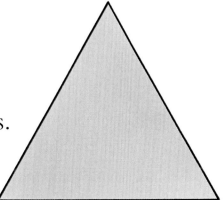

Then use all six cards to make a hexagon.

What is a pyramid?

A triangle is a flat shape. A solid triangle is called a pyramid.

There are two types of pyramid. A square pyramid is a solid shape with five faces. Four of the faces are triangles. The fifth face is a square. The square face forms the base of the pyramid.

A triangular pyramid has four triangle-shaped faces of the same size. This shape is called a tetrahedron.

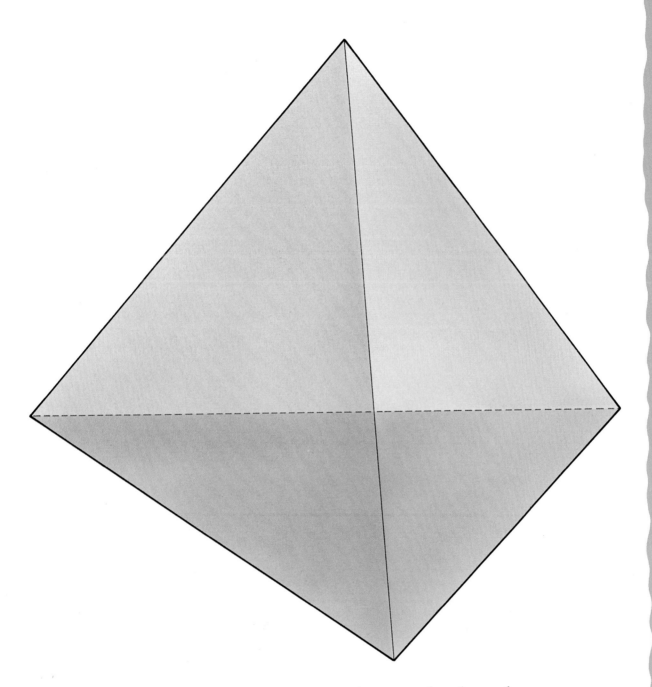

Pyramids of the same size can be stacked up because they fit neatly together. Many small pyramids can be used to form one large pyramid.

Triangles around us

Triangles are common shapes and they have many uses.

There is a musical instrument called a triangle. It is a metal rod that is bent so that it has three sides. Different notes are produced by tapping it in different places.

A photographer often **supports** a camera on a tripod. A tripod has three legs. The legs make the same shape as a triangular pyramid. This shape is difficult to knock over. ▼

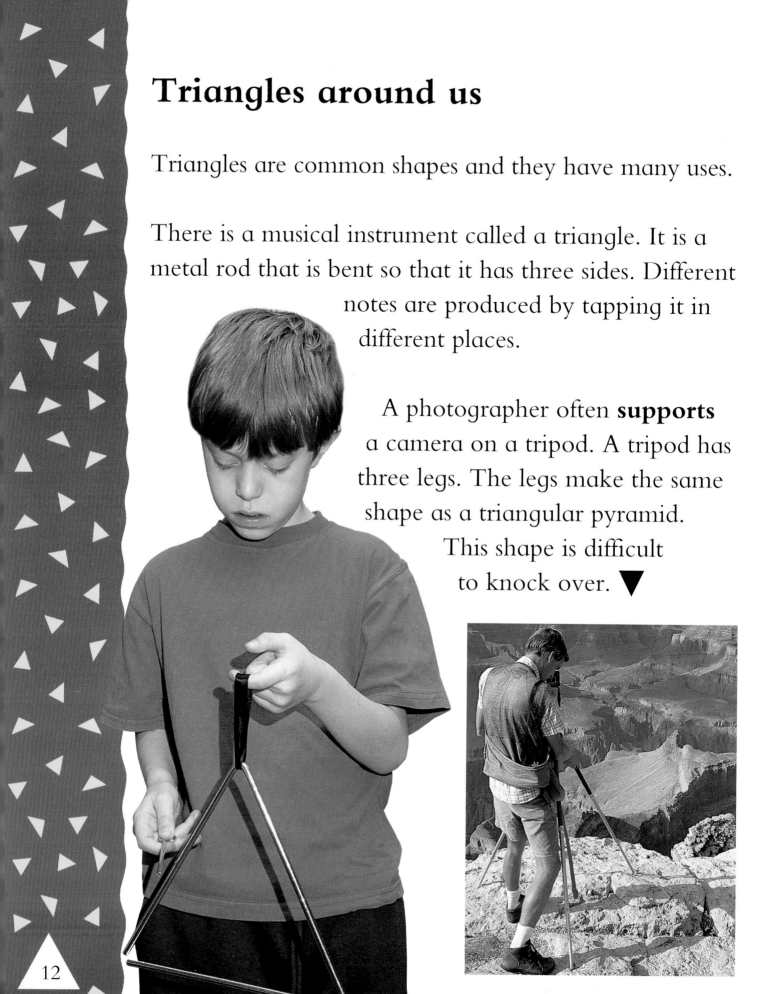

Surveyors use a ▶ tripod to keep their **theodolite** steady. They use the theodolite to take measurements.

DANGER OF DEATH KEEP OUT

◀ Road signs come in many shapes. The triangular signs often have a red edge. They are **warning** signs. This sign warns people about the danger of electricity.

There are three signs on this ▶ post. The triangular sign is a warning that the road ahead may be slippery. The other two signs warn that there may be rain or snow.

Moving triangles

Many things that can fly in the air or sail on the water have a triangular shape.

◀ Sails on boats are made from a triangle of material. The sails are held up in the air.

When the wind hits the sails, it moves the boat. Sailors can control the speed at which the boat moves by opening or closing the sails. To change direction, they have to move the sails.

Windsurfers use a single large sail attached to a special board. The windsurfer holds on to the sail and moves it around to catch the wind. They have to **balance** very carefully on the board, otherwise they will fall off!

Hang-gliders, too, use a single triangular piece of material. The triangle forms a wing and catches the wind. Hang-gliders glide gracefully and quietly through the air.

Aeroplanes also use triangular wings to fly. This aeroplane is a Concorde.

A fish has a powerful tail to help it swim through water. It uses its fins to change direction and to control its swimming movements. This shark has several fins that are triangular in shape.

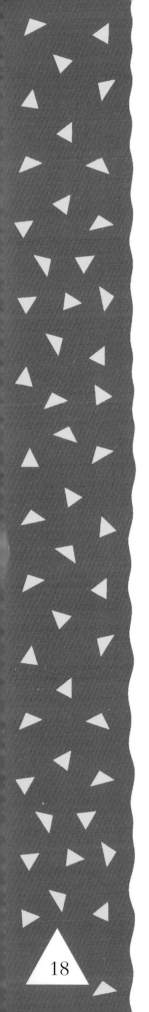

Triangles within triangles

Many of the **structures** that we see around us every day are made from small triangles.

This is a picture of a washing line photographed from above. There is a big triangle on the outside and smaller ones inside.

Pylons hold up electricity **cables**. If you look closely, you will see that they are made up of lots of small triangles joined together.

Tower cranes are built in a similar way to electricity pylons. Tower cranes are found on building sites, where they lift heavy objects and move them around.

Triangles are strong

The triangle is a very stable shape. This makes it useful for building things like bridges or roofs.

Often you see steel poles around buildings that are being repaired. This is called scaffolding. It helps the builders to move materials around the building and to reach the upper floors. You can see many triangular shapes in this scaffolding. The triangles help to make the scaffolding strong and safe.

This is a **girder** bridge. The iron rods have been arranged in triangles to give the bridge strength. Heavy vehicles can cross this bridge safely.

We make use of triangles when we put up tents and teepees. Ropes are used to hold them in place. Teepees form a triangular shape.

Heavy cables are often used to support roofs. This building is in Spain. The roof acts as a huge tent, supported by many strong cables. The cables make a triangular shape.

Natural triangles

There are not many examples of natural triangles.
However, many four-legged animals seem to make
triangular shapes when they move.

Look carefully at the legs of these elephants as they
walk. When their legs move forward, they form
a natural triangle. Animals with four legs have to move
their legs carefully so that they keep their balance all
the time.

The giraffe is a very tall animal and can reach the leaves on the higher branches of trees. However, when it wants to drink the giraffe has to bend its neck to bring its mouth to the water. To do this, the giraffe spreads its front legs to make a triangle. This shape is stable, and so the giraffe does not topple forward into the water.

Famous triangles and pyramids

◄ The Eiffel Tower is a very famous tower in Paris, the capital city of France. It has a triangular shape made up of many smaller triangles. The Eiffel Tower is made of iron. It was built over a hundred years ago.

The most famous pyramid shapes in the world are the ancient pyramids in Egypt. They are just outside the capital city, Cairo. These pyramids were built many thousands of years ago as **tombs** for the pharaohs, the kings of Egypt. ▼

San Francisco in the USA has many tall buildings. One of these skyscrapers, the Trans American building, has been built in the shape of a pyramid. At the bottom of the building, triangles help to support it. ▶

In Paris there is a well-known art gallery called the Louvre. In front of this gallery there is a modern pyramid made of metal and glass. ▼

Make a pyramid

Trace the shape below on to a piece of card and cut it out.

Fold the shape as marked on the diagram. Then put glue on the flaps. Stick each flap to the flap next to it.

You have made a square pyramid with five faces. Four of the faces are triangles, but the fifth face is square.

Other shapes

Look carefully at the pattern below. See how many triangles you can find. You may be able to find a square too.

This is a photograph of a cathedral in the Italian city of Siena. Look carefully at the decorated walls. There are lots of different shapes.

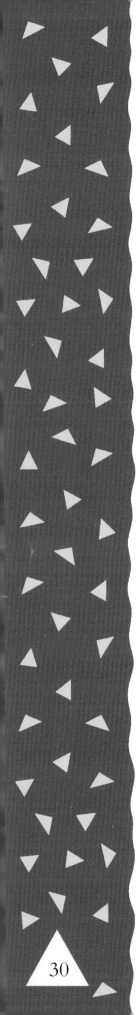

Glossary

Balance Keep steady.

Cables Thick ropes or lengths of metal.

Differ Be different.

Girder A beam of wood, iron or steel.

Structures Buildings, or things that are built.

Supports Holds up.

Surveyors People who make careful examinations of land or buildings.

Theodolite A measuring instrument used by surveyors.

Tombs Graves.

Warning Something that shows that danger is nearby.

Books to read

Circles and Spheres by Sally Morgan (Wayland, 1994)

Shape by Richard Hales and Nicky Hales (Cherrytree, 1991)

Shapes by Jacqueline Dineen (Wayland, 1990)

Shapes by John Satchwell (Walker, 1988)

Spirals by Sally Morgan (Wayland, 1994)

Squares and Cubes by Sally Morgan (Wayland, 1994)

Picture acknowledgements

The publishers wish to thank the following for providing the pictures for this book: Biofotos 22; Chapel Studios 7 (Zul Mukhida), 12 (left, Zul Mukhida), 13 (top, John Heinrich), 17 (top, Reuben Beckett); Bruce Coleman Limited 23 (M. P. Kahl); Ecoscene 6-7 (Gryniewicz), 13 (left, Nick Hawkes; bottom right, Morgan), 16 (left, Towse), 18 (top, Anthony Cooper), 21 (bottom, Groves), 28 (Morgan); Eye Ubiquitous 4 (left, Peter Blake), 12 (right, L. Johnstone), 25 (left, Paul Seheult); Hutchison 14 (left, Nancy Durrell McKenna), 25 (right, Bernard Régent); Impact 4 (right, Simon Shepheard), 19 (Mike McQueen); Photri 18 (bottom, B. Howe), 20 (top, Mike Boroff); Tony Stone Worldwide 14-15 (Warren Bolster); Wayland Picture Library cover, 9, 27; ZEFA 6 (left), 17 (bottom), 20 (bottom), 21 (top), 24 (both).
Artwork by Peter Bull.

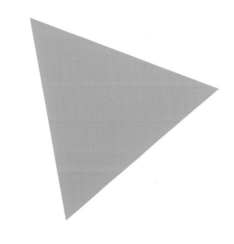

Index